A SHADOW OF HERSELF

A true story of mental illness, courage, and love

Diane Lehnig

When mental illness strikes a beautiful teenage girl, she and her family struggle to accept the disease. The journey is both frightening and heartbreaking as tragic events unfold. This true biography shares the innermost thoughts of Shannon as she faces the demons that are in her head.

DIANE LEHNIG

A SHADOW OF HERSELF

A true story of mental illness, courage, and love

This book is dedicated to my daughter, one of the strongest women I know, and to my family , especially my husband Tom, and my grandson Martin. I cannot forget to thank God. The footprints in the sand were very deep as He carried all four of us on the journey.

Note: Some names and dates have been changed to protect those people mentioned in the story.

It is my hope that this story will be an inspiration for all patients and their families who struggle with mental illness, and for all who seek to treat the illness.

DIANE LEHNIG

CHAPTER ONE

Shannon could have killed my grandson that day in 2008. The thoughts that some of us hear when a misbehaving child won't listen, the thoughts that say, "I want to kill him," those thoughts for most are just small, whispering voices that are immediately quieted by reason and rational thoughts.

For my daughter, they were not just thoughts but voices, and the voices were loud. They told her,

He hates you! You're ugly! He needs to die.

The more she was with Martin that day, the more insistent the voices became.

She dressed her son in little shorts and a clean shirt. He was crying. The crying became louder and louder, and the voices more insistent. She lit a cigarette, hoping the nicotine would quell the voices into whispers that she could no longer hear.

"Let's go to the creek," she said. He smiled. But to her, it was an evil smile. He ran down the path toward the creek. "Martin, get back here!" When she called her little four-year-old, he ran away from her.

He hates you. You're a bitch. You're never going to be a good mother.

When they arrived at the creek, he played in the shallow end of a deep pool, turning over rocks, looking for salamanders and tadpoles. The voices commanded her to lure him into the deeper part of the creek, but he was content to stay in the clear running water.

Their little dog, Newton, had followed them to the creek. Picking up the dog, she threw him into the deep water. Martin turned and waded toward the little dog that was struggling to climb the muddy bank.

It would be so easy.

Distracted by a dragonfly, Martin turned back toward the shore. "Mommy, look at the bugs," he squealed as Newton managed to scramble on to the grass. Picking up a large rock in her left hand, she walked over to Martin.

Hit him, hit him.

She stood there, frozen, the heavy rock suspended above her son's head.

Do it. Do it now.

*S*ince Martin had been born, every day had been a struggle for Shannon. He was an active child, one that required so much of her time and energy. She was doing her best to raise her son, reading books on child-rearing and childhood behavior. All the while, as the months passed, the voices grew in frequency and strength. The voices were unrelenting. She knew it was an awful thing to hurt a child. But to whom should she listen? The voices? The books? Her parents?

"Mommy, why are you crying?" Martin's voice penetrated through the voices, and at that moment, a wave of reality washed into her thoughts. She dropped the rock, picked up Martin, and carried him home. He was tired, and she hoped he would take a long nap. Soon I would be home from work. Then she, Shannon, could also take a nap.

That evening, while I prepared dinner, my daughter sat in a chair, staring at her hands. "Mom, he needs to go to daycare tomorrow. I'm afraid I'm going to hurt him," she said.

The lack of expression on her face told me I needed to act immediately. So the next morning, I enrolled Martin in daycare.

Much later, many years later, she told me she had tried to kill him that day.

He does not know. He only remembers wonderful trips to the creek with his mother before she got too sick to take him anywhere. Although her voices were loud, although they told her she had to hurt him that day, the reality was she was a twenty-eight-year-old mother who took her child to the creek and then put him to bed for a nap.

2

The voices were always there; as long as she could remember, they had told her what to do, how to think, what to say. But throughout her childhood, and in her early teenage years, they were softer. Shannon could usually push them away by listening to music, watching TV, or playing with her brothers.

"Mom, they're all laughing at me. Everybody tells me I'm ugly," she told me one night in 1996 when she was sixteen.

I remember just brushing her words aside, "Don't listen to them. You're very pretty." I knew that teenage girls could be very cruel to each other. "They're just jealous because you are so tall and beautiful, and very smart, too."

I wish I had known then what I know now. But would it have made any difference?

At the age of 17, my daughter got her first job, working at a truck stop in Erie, Pennsylvania. In the beginning, she was always laughing and joking with the truckers. They called her "the skinny little bitch." She loved the teasing, even attaching a bumper sticker with that quote to her car.

At first, she loved the job, her independence, and the paycheck too. But then, one day, the voices became more persuasive and the panic attacks started. She couldn't breathe; she said she was suffocating, her chest felt heavy; her coworkers called 911.

You're a rotten cashier; your boyfriend is cheating on you.

A few weeks later they had to call 911 again.

You're ugly and too tall to be a girl; you don't even have boobs.

And then a few weeks later it happened again. The doctors at the Emergency Room diagnosed her with panic attacks and anxiety.

Everyone's staring at you; your clothes don't fit right; you're really stupid.

"Shannon, what is going on?" I asked her. "Maybe your hormones are just out of whack. Do you think you need to see a doctor?"

"I need a boob job," she told me.

"What? What does that have to do with panic attacks?"

"I'm ugly. You would panic, too, if everyone called you names and told you that you looked like a man. And they're right; just look at me, I'm so flat. I don't even look like a girl. "

That was hard for us to believe. Tall and slender, with a small nose, high cheekbones, and Barbie Doll legs, she looked like a model on the cover of *Vogue*. Shannon was smart, had four or five close friends, and often hung out with the boy next door, who was enamored with her looks and her sense of humor.

But Shannon was insistent. "You don't know what it's like, Mom. You were always beautiful, but I am not."

Tom, Shannon's stepfather, and I disagreed with her. "First of all, breast enhancement is too expensive, and second of all, you don't need it," we told her.

They don't love you. Just look in the mirror and you'll see how deformed you are. If they loved you, they'd pay for the surgery.

Sobbing, one evening after school, Shannon shrieked, "You don't care that I'm ugly. I'm deformed!" She ran to her room and slammed the door.

Later that night, after Shannon crept out of her bedroom, I sat on the couch with her. "Shannon, you are not deformed. Look in the mirror! Look at all the girls in your school. Who would you rather look like, you or them?"

"Mom, they all say I'm ugly, that I look like a man. I don't want to go to school anymore; everyone laughs at me." Shannon was crying again. No matter what we said, or how many times we told her how beautiful and smart she was, she insisted she needed surgery.

"It must be terrible to be made fun of," I told Tom. "What do you think we should we do?"

Tom was mostly confused by Shannon's behavior and had few significant suggestions.

At night, I wept. How could anyone be so cruel, I thought? The school shouldn't allow such bullying. My beautiful daughter was in pain. The kids at school made fun of her, and because she didn't know their names, I couldn't even report it.

After weeks of arguing and tears and 'I hate you,' Tom and I gave in, and I made an appointment to take Shannon to a plastic surgeon.

We found out that the outpatient surgery for breast enhancement would be around $5000. I was working as a registered nurse at the time, and Tom was a sheet metal journeyman. Having been married before, Tom was paying 30% of his paycheck to support his two young children from a previous marriage. Between the two of us, we had six children, including one in art school and another at a local college. Money was tight.

The day of the appointment finally arrived. Shannon was very cheerful thinking about her new perfect body. She chattered and laughed in the car while we traveled to the appointment.

That happiness was short-lived. After checking Shannon's breasts, the surgeon gave his opinion: "You don't need plastic surgery," he told her. "Your breasts are still growing, and we hesitate to operate on someone who is so young."

Your mom must have bribed him to say that. Everyone is out to get you. You're ugly. No one likes you.

"You don't know what it's like! Everyone makes fun of me. I'm ugly!" Shannon ran out of the office.

In the days following that appointment, Shannon began calling in sick to her after-school job. She slept more and more. She didn't want to go out with her friends, and she often skipped school when we were at work. Finally, she quit her job.

In a few months' time, Shannon's health declined. She had constant headaches, her appetite decreased, she lost weight. Every night I prayed that God would help Shannon recognize her beauty. It seemed as if Shannon was not capable of living in reality. Her vision of herself seemed very warped.

Your mother's worried that your stepfather will think you're more attractive than she is. That's why she won't let you have the surgery. Your mother's jealous of you.

Concerned about Shannon's health and attitude, I made an appointment for her with our family physician. After the examination and blood work, he informed us that Shannon was probably suffering from depression. In February of Shannon's junior year in high school, she started taking the medication Paxil, an antidepressant.

Depression. We were relieved to hear that diagnosis. We knew about depression. It ran in my family. Both of my grandmothers and my mother had been treated for depression. And I had struggled with that in the past. It was treatable. Everything would be okay. It was an acceptable diagnosis, something our family members could understand.

There was other mental illness in the family, too. My great-grandmother had had a "nervous breakdown" when she had been in her forties. She had lost all contact with reality, not recognizing family members and not remembering her past. She had spent the last 30 years of her life in an institution with a diagnosis of schizophrenia. But her life was different, I told myself. She had lost an infant daughter to meningitis, a 16-year-old daughter to heart disease, and her oldest son to a bullet in World War I. All of those tragedies had pushed her over the edge. And in the early 1900's there were few options to treat the condition.

My daughter did not have those life situations. And I convinced myself that my daughter did not have that mental illness. My daughter had depression: There were lots of medications and treatments. Shannon would be fine once the meds started to work.

And they did. Shannon started singing and going out with her friends again; her outbursts lessened in frequency. Throughout the depression, Shannon had been sporadically attending high school. When the Paxil began to work, she began to thrive. She got a different job, again working as a cashier. She went to her Junior Prom, and a year later, to her Senior Prom. The voices seemed to fade as the medication got into her system.

In 1998, while in her senior year of high school, Shannon applied for college. She was accepted at Penn State Behrend in our hometown of Erie, Pennsylvania. Her two older brothers were getting As and Bs in college. Her younger brother, George, was enjoying life in a technical high school. Tom's children were both still in middle school and thriving.

We were so proud, living the American Dream, bragging about our amazing children. For that brief period, we were standing in the bright light of life, unaware of the dark journey that would soon follow.

3

Shannon entered college in the fall of 1998. Unlike high school where tall, slender girls were sometimes ridiculed and called "string bean," college men liked tall, thin girls. She started dating: many dates with many different boys. She was on the internet constantly, posting sexy pictures of herself. Every day was exciting as she started to realize she was pretty and nice and smart. Phone calls were almost always for her. We couldn't keep track of the many men she was dating.

She was in her second semester of her freshman year of college when the voices returned with a vengeance. This time, they would not be quieted with Paxil.

Everyone is looking at you. See that girl over there who's whispering to her friend? She says you're ugly and stupid.

"I AM NOT!" shouted Shannon. The outburst happened right in the middle of class. Shannon ran out of the classroom.

"I hate college. I thought college kids would be more mature, but they're not. They're all mean to me. They tell me I'm too stupid to go to college."

"There are mean people in this world," I said. "Focus on the good people, ignore the bad ones."

It was probably the stress of college that brought back the depression, I thought. I wanted to know the names of the people who said the terrible and mean things to Shannon. But again Shannon said she didn't know who they were.

During the many conversations with Shannon, we heard about mean people, about how ugly she was, about what she needed, and about what would make her happy. She overwhelmed us with her need for money to fix the problems. The conversations typically ended with yelling or crying. Tom was especially frustrated, as Shannon would take out her anger on him, calling him names and ignoring his comments and questions.

At night, Tom and I sat up talking about the egocentric spoiled-brat child we were raising. Was it the divorce that made her so self-centered? Behind her back, we started calling her the psychic vampire. Some days it felt as if our happiness was being drained from our bodies. Whenever she was in the room, the conversation was always about her and her problems. Many nights, we would go to bed exhausted from the conflicts.

I remember one day when we were in Walmart and Shannon started screaming at an overweight woman who was standing in line. "How dare you call me ugly, you fat bitch?"

I hurried out of the store. "I'm not going to take you shopping anymore if you're going to act like that. You embarrassed me!"

"She started it!" Shannon yelled. "She called me names, so I let her have it!"

Your Mom must be deaf if she didn't hear that fat bitch. She called you an ugly whore. No one is on your side. Your mother is a bitch, too.

Shannon made the Dean's list during her first semester at college then flunked out the next.

Desperate to make friends and fit in, she began going to parties where there was easy access to street drugs. Ecstasy and marijuana were her favorites. Loud music drowned out the voices and the ecstasy made her feel like she was pretty. We worried about the downward spiral of changes we were witnessing. Discovering marijuana and some unknown pills in her dresser one day, we demanded that Shannon stop using them. I was convinced that the drugs were the reason that Shannon had dropped out of college.

Your parents are jerks. Your mother hates you because you are having fun. Your stepfather listens to your mother. You should move out. You need a life!

"You're a fucking bitch! Did you know your husband told me I was ugly when you were at work? How does that feel?" she screamed at me one afternoon.

I was stunned. I thought I had been a good mother. I knew Tom would never hurt Shannon, or did I? I couldn't believe this girl that I loved so much could say such hurtful things. I started to cry.

"You're such a fake. Do you think tears will make me feel sorry for you? You never loved me. And I certainly don't love you," she said.

Shannon decided that the voices were right. She needed to get away from her controlling, nagging parents. She was working at the truck stop again and decided to move out.

4

Shannon found an apartment near her work and moved out of our house. First she lived with a girlfriend, and then with a boyfriend, and then with a different boyfriend. For a while, she didn't visit us very often. We sporadically kept in touch by phone. After each broken relationship, Shannon would find a new boyfriend. No relationship was ever good enough. She would get tired of the relationships, tired of the men.

It seemed like each boyfriend was a step down from the previous one. She moved in with drug addicts and unemployed men. She would go to her job to support them; they would stay at their apartments, smoke weed, and play video games.

The men aren't the problem. You are the problem. No man with a job would ever want to be around you.

At the end of each relationship, Shannon would be either hysterical and broken-hearted or relieved. Some of her ex-boyfriends refused to accept the end of the parasitic bond. A few stalked her, requiring Tom, my ex-husband, or one of her brothers to intervene. Others would cry, trying to shame her into continuing the relationship.

"Why do you end up with these men?" I asked. "They're not good for you. You're much too smart. "Maybe you should think about going back to college."

"Oh, Jesus! Give me a break! I hated college," she answered.

In 2000, when Shannon was 20 years old, Tom and I bought an old farmhouse in New York, only a few miles from Erie, and moved out of Pennsylvania. The house had five bedrooms, and since Shannon could no longer afford her apartment, she moved in with us.

It didn't take long before Tom and I were constantly arguing about Shannon and her behavior. Of course, I knew it was because she was MY daughter and not his. His daughter was short and blond and perfect. She was getting straight As in school and was popular and happy. MY daughter was distraught, thought she was ugly at times, and took it out on us. It was understandable that Shannon would act out. I told Tom he had to treat Shannon the way he treated his daughter.

Tom and I rarely argued; then when Shannon moved back in, her behaviors caused constant friction. Her conduct became the focus of our lives.

Then one day in 2002, while on a dating site, Shannon started chatting with 'Aaron,' who lived four hours away in State College, Pennsylvania.

"Aaron's smart," Shannon told me. "He's working as a computer analyst."

We didn't even know if that was the truth. We had heard about her smart, talented boyfriends before, and they always ended up quitting their jobs while Shannon worked to supply them with their needed marijuana and alcohol.

After chatting with Aaron for several weeks, Shannon decided to visit him. We were terrified that Shannon might be getting involved with another unemployed addict, and tried to convince her that she should be cautious. We had read and heard many stories about young women getting raped or killed after meeting someone online. But there was no stopping her.

She left for a four-day visit with Aaron in September, 2002. Whenever she left our house, even for brief excursions, Tom and I would relax and have fun together. Whenever Shannon was living with us, her irrational behavior brought constant problems to our marriage.

She decided she was in love. After returning home, she informed us that she was moving away to live with

Aaron. On one hand, we were worried about her leaving. On the other hand, it was quite a relief to have her gone. Later, after she left, that relief turned into guilt because we felt we were tossing our daughter out into the dangerous world.

He loves you. He'll take care of you. He doesn't see how ugly you are. He thinks you're pretty. He just loves you for you. No one has ever loved you like this before.

Aaron was a skinny, very intelligent man, about an inch shorter than Shannon. He had a great job, making excellent money working for Accuweather. He had studied to become an aeronautics engineer but had ruined his chances in that career when a drug test had come up positive for marijuana.

Although Shannon seemed to enjoy his company, her brothers, especially George, couldn't stand him. When we asked George why he didn't like Aaron, his answer was vague. "He's a whiney little man," George said.

Shannon started working for a veterinarian in State College. She immediately adopted a cat with serious health problems: seizures. One day the cat got out of the house, ran into oncoming traffic, and was severely injured. Shannon spent over $500 trying to save the cat, which died a few days later. Because she was not making much money working for the vet, we sent her money.

Visiting her and Aaron in State College often cost us hundreds of dollars. Shannon would cry because her clothes didn't fit her, so I would take her shopping, hoping that nicer clothes would help her feel better about herself.

It was ironic. I was working as a registered nurse, and would only spend a few dollars on pants from the Salvation Army. One pair of jeans for Shannon, who was working as a vet tech, cost me over $40.

In the end, the relationship with Aaron proved to be toxic. Aaron, who struggled with social situations, and who had been abused by his father, was heavily into mind-altering drugs. Shannon willingly jumped into that lifestyle. The decline in her mental state reflected the increased drug use.

How could anyone love you? Your boobs never grew. That doctor lied to you. Everyone lies to you.

After only six months living with Aaron, Shannon decided she wanted to come home. Unwilling to have our life in chaos again, we told her we'd help her find an apartment near us. Aaron, who was quite fascinated with Shannon, told Shannon he was moving with her and quit his job to follow her.

Unaware of Aaron's drug problem, we helped Shannon and Aaron find an apartment in the small town of

Westfield, New York, in May, 2003. We paid the first month's rent to help them get on their feet.

"A boob job would make you look better, and your clothes would fit better, too," Aaron told her.

Finally, someone believes that you need surgery.

Without our knowledge, rather than looking for a job, Shannon immediately found a doctor who would enhance her breasts. It was a painful surgery. She wouldn't leave the apartment for weeks, and the pain medications made her sick. But when she looked in the mirror, she finally saw a girl, a woman.

You look good for the first time in your life. Now you will be happy.

Aaron, of course, was quite happy with his large-breasted girlfriend. We had hoped that he would find a job in the area to help pay the rent. That didn't happen. He sat at home, smoking weed and playing on their newly-purchased computer.

Shannon was out of money and now had a huge bill from a credit card that had paid for not only her surgery, but also the computer. She took a nurse's aide course at a local nursing home and began working forty hours a week to support herself and Aaron.

She tolerated the job but said she felt sorry for the residents in the nursing home. She didn't have enough time to spend with them, and the heavy lifting hurt her back. She also began smoking, mostly to fit in with the other aides, she said.

After seven months of living in Westfield, Aaron still didn't have a job. They decided that the problem must be their location. They broke the lease and Shannon and Aaron moved to Pittsburgh, Pennsylvania. This time, Shannon's father paid the deposit and the first month's rent on their apartment.

Getting a job seemed unimportant to them. They spent their days smoking pot and their nights going to raves. Neither one found a job. They maxed out Shannon's credit card.

Then the panic attacks started again. Often Shannon would call us, crying about having no money and not being able to find a job. Tom and I decided throwing money at Shannon had helped create the problem, so we refused to send her any more.

Our fourth child, George, was in college by this time. He was in an apprenticeship program in Pittsburgh, about half an hour from where Shannon and Aaron were living. I asked him to check on Shannon, but she wouldn't answer his repeated phone calls. George had had no problem in the past telling his sister how much he disliked Aaron.

When she would call us, which was rare, I would encourage her to leave Aaron, but she would refuse, saying that Aaron would kill himself if she did. Not knowing what to do, I prayed, "Please find a way to bring Shannon home before she ends up dead."

Shannon was now off her anti-depressant medications, as she could no longer afford to pay for them. She was 23 years old with no job and massive credit card debt. Her conversations were bizarre: crying one minute and laughing hysterically the next. I was sure the depression was back again.

Then one afternoon, I received a call from George. He had been in the emergency room in Pittsburgh, diagnosed with kidney stones. He needed to come home, but couldn't drive because of the pain.

I called Shannon, who for once answered the phone. "Your brother is in pain and needs to come home. Could you please go to his school and pick him up? He's too ill to drive."

She immediately agreed, drove to George's school and brought him to our home. Once home, she decided to stay and not to go back to Pittsburgh.

At first, Aaron was furious, and then said he couldn't live without Shannon. He called her up, crying and sobbing, threatening to kill himself if she wouldn't come back to him. Later that month, Shannon's father and George drove to Pittsburgh to retrieve Shannon's clothes and George's car. Because Shannon felt sorry for Aaron, she told her dad to leave the computer. They warned Aaron to stay away from her.

Shannon stopped answering Aaron's phone calls. Not to be deterred, Aaron showed up at our house. Shannon was a mental disaster by this time. And the voices that had once told her that he would save her now told her that he was the problem.

It's his fault. He didn't love you. He said you looked like a man, even with your boob job. You were always too tall for him.

Tom and I decided to send Shannon out of the state to get away from Aaron. In January, 2004, we bought her a plane ticket, and she flew out to Colorado to stay with my brother for a few months.

When she returned, Aaron had disappeared. Broke and broken, Shannon again moved in with us.

Shannon's father paid off some of her credit card bills. Paying off Shannon's debts was one of many mistakes we would all make to try to keep Shannon happy. We knew what enabling was, but failed to identify our behavior as such. None of us were aware that we were only putting a Band-Aid on a gaping wound that would eventually require many stitches.

Shannon got another job, this time at a fireworks store as a cashier. She went back on Paxil, and for a while, lived with us again. It wasn't long before she started dating again, sometimes as many as three dates in the same week. Flowers arrived at the house after some dates. They loved her. She was funny, she was cute, she was smart, and she had big boobs. Although Shannon lived with us full-time, she wasn't home much. Our lives were relatively stable for the next couple of years.

We were happy because she was happy. But "And they all lived happily ever after" was not to be our future.

5

It all changed the summer of 2004 when Shannon met another man online who was tall, dark, and handsome. 'Eric' didn't have a job because he had seizures, he said. He worked off the books, caring for a disabled woman. At the time, Eric was living in Scranton, PA, six hours from Shannon.

One weekend he got a ride up to Erie, PA, not just to visit Shannon, but also to visit his family. Shannon and Eric went to the local amusement park that Saturday evening.

She told me that he had cried when the day had been over because he had never had such a good time in his whole life. They spent most of that weekend together.

Although Eric lived six hours from her, he phoned Shannon every day. Some weekends, she would drive to Scranton to see him. They went on picnics. They went on long walks together.

Meanwhile, Shannon was dating two other men at the same time. She went out to dinner and the movies; she went fishing and swimming. She was working again and had money in the bank. It seemed like she was laughing all the time. Her world was exciting and happy. She felt pretty.

"I'm pregnant."

6

We weren't sure who the father was, but Shannon said she knew. She stopped going out with everyone except for Eric. He seemed very excited to be having a child. She immediately said she wasn't going to take any chances with her baby's health. Birth defects were listed as possible side-effects of most of Shannon's meds. Knowing that any medication could be harmful to a fetus, we agreed with Shannon. But Tom and I were nervous.

After she found out she was pregnant, Shannon saw Eric frequently; sometimes she would drive to Scranton, sometimes he would find a ride to visit her. He was quite a handsome man, 6-foot-2 with dark hair and dark eyes. He told us he couldn't drive because of the seizures and was trying to get social security disability.

Shannon and Eric decided they needed to live together, to raise their child. This time, instead of finding an apartment or moving in with us, Shannon moved in with Eric and his parents in Erie, Pennsylvania. Growing up,

Shannon had been used to a clean house, family dinners together in the evenings, church on Sundays, and for the most part, family members who got along with each other.

With this move, she was exposed to a life far different from anything she had previously experienced. Not only were alcohol and street drugs in abundance, but family members shared prescription drugs, too. It was a world where stealing from a store or a job was not only permitted, but encouraged. Fistfights were common, verbal fights frequent. There were no family meals; the occupants ate at fast-food restaurants, and when the money ran out, they would stand in line at the food banks for free food. The home was filled with trash bags and infested with fleas.

At first, Shannon seemed happy, even under those conditions, and looked forward to being treated as a special person because she was pregnant. And at first, Eric was a wonderfully supportive partner. He continued to be thrilled that he was going to be a father.

Then one morning, for no apparent reason, Eric started with the verbal bashing. "You're a bitch, you're ugly, and you're fat." These were not voices; these were real. These words were spewing out of the Eric's mouth.

As her pregnancy progressed, Shannon began to realize he did not have seizures; he was mentally ill. He heard voices; he had hallucinations. He ducked when nonexistent objects attacked him. He couldn't drive; he couldn't work. He didn't take his medications as prescribed, and he frequently drank alcohol and smoked pot while on powerful prescription drugs.

Shannon and Eric arrived at our house with a car full of chrysanthemums one afternoon. They planted a few of the flowers around our mailbox.

"How thoughtful," I exclaimed.

"We stole them from Kmart. Just drove right up there when the store was closed and threw them in the trunk," Shannon laughingly advised me. "You should see the other stuff we got!"

I was horrified. She thought it was funny.

She was pregnant and working, and she had to take care of Eric, too. He had psychotic episodes when everything went dark and he woke up not remembering anything. He encouraged Shannon to take his medications, to help keep her calm. But she refused, worried about the effects on her unborn child.

Martin was born one evening in early April, 2005. Eric and I were both there when baby Martin arrived. I cried as I held that precious, beautiful baby boy. But something was wrong with Shannon. She didn't want to hold her newborn son; she didn't even want to look at him.

You'll never be a good mother; you can't even nurse him because of your fake boobs. Look how much he cries. He hates you.

But she did nurse him. She told me she loved him more than anyone she had loved before. She wept because of the powerful emotions she felt. Her boyfriend, Eric, said she spoiled Martin, and told Shannon not to pick him up when he cried. Eric said he wanted Martin to grow up to be tough. Shannon knew she should pick him up and cuddle him. But Eric said "NO!" Alone in his crib, Martin wailed. Feeling confused and alone, Shannon felt like her head was exploding. So she cried and cried.

Angry at both of them, Eric held out his medication-filled hand, and Shannon took Eric's medications that she had refused so many times before. She didn't know what to do. At least the pills numbed the strong feelings and allowed her to sleep while Martin cried.

He hates you.

Martin had trouble nursing, often sucking in air instead of the breast milk; he had colic and he fussed day and night. She would sometimes bring him to our house, where I would rock him and sing to him while Shannon tried to get some rest.

He likes her better than you. He hates you. You should have never had a baby. You don't know how to take care of him.

One day, in February of 2006, nothing seemed to stop Martin's crying. He threw his bottle; he wouldn't sleep, he spit out his food. She sat him in his baby walker, which usually stopped the screeching. But the noise didn't stop.

He's crying because he doesn't like you. Babies don't cry when they love their mothers. You are a rotten mother.

Standing in the kitchen, she clapped her hands over her ears to stop the voices. But they were adamant. Shannon ran down to the basement to put in a load of laundry. Distracted by the voices, she forgot to close the door after she climbed back up the stairs.

He hates you. He wanted a mother, and you look like a man. You are too ugly to be a woman.

Shannon walked into the living room trying to get away from the voices, leaving baby Martin, still in his walker, alone in the kitchen.

From the basement stairwell came a noise. The walker was falling down those stairs--a walker with a baby in it.

Down he went, each stair bumping the walker. She screamed as she heard the sound.

Sobbing and screaming, she ran to the stairs, expecting to see his broken little body. How could she be so evil, killing her son?

I told Shannon that angels must have carried him down the stairs that day. In spite of falling down fourteen steps, the walker never tipped over, and Martin was unhurt. She told me she threw out the walker so he could never fall like that again.

The situation with Eric continued to get worse. Eric would go out at night to play cards, or go to the local casinos, and leave her alone with the baby. Sometimes he wouldn't come home at all. Eric started making up reasons why he couldn't come home. She suspected he was seeing other women.

One night he arrived home very late in a drug-induced state. He told her that he had been sexually abused by his father and was seeing a counselor in the evenings. But by this time, Shannon didn't believe anything he said.

She was working evenings, bringing the baby over to our house in nearby New York State. Eric sat at home or went out drinking, telling us he couldn't watch Martin. He was having too many seizures and was afraid he'd drop Martin, he said.

It was April, soon after the almost-tragedy with the walker, when Eric told us about Shannon's odd activities and strange remarks.

"She changes her clothes five or six times a day," Eric told me over the phone. "She says nothing fits! She's crying a lot and says she wants to give Martin up for adoption. She says she's afraid she'll hurt him."

When we asked Shannon what was going on, she repeated many of the same phrases we had heard years before. "They all say I'm ugly! Look at me, I look like a man! Martin hates me!"

Tom and I knew that Shannon needed to get away from Eric. But we wanted to avoid having Shannon move back in with us again. I knew the chaos that would follow. Although she was obviously upset most of the time, I didn't want the pandemonium again. And this time, she would be bringing a baby with her.

By this time, she wasn't bathing, or bathing Martin. She started wearing clothes that were too big for her. She cut off her long, beautiful dark hair.

Finally, afraid that either she or Martin would be injured, we told her to move back in with us.

We put on a brave face in public and joked about the situation, telling people we had a yo-yo daughter. She moved in, then she moved out, then she moved in again. We made it sound funny, but there was very little laughter in our house as her actions continued the downward spiral.

You need to give him up for adoption. You were happy before he was born. You'll never be a good mother. Your mother takes care of him. You can't. You're a failure.

Shannon began staring at the mirror, at the floor, and sometimes, it seemed, at nothing. She often didn't hear us when we talked to her. She smoked constantly.

She would get up with the baby in the morning before I went to work, but I cared for him whenever I was home, including nights. When I realized she wasn't getting up with him when he cried at night, I moved his crib into our bedroom so I could get up with him.

When I was at work, Shannon would fix Martin's breakfast and then bring his high chair into the living room. Later I learned he'd sit there most of the morning, watching cartoons.

Your mother never wanted you. She hates girls. She wanted all boys. Now she wants your son.

We noticed it seemed to take all of Shannon's energy just to change his diapers and feed him. I wasn't sure how much time Shannon was spending in the house with him. We would come home to a pile of cigarette butts scattered on the porch and on the driveway. She rarely helped with the housework, although she still did her laundry. She refused to clean up the cigarette butts. She didn't help with meals, but would immediately hand Martin to me when I got home from work and then run out to smoke again. After supper, she would go upstairs to her room.

Tom and I saw less and less of each other, as my caring for Martin took more and more of my time. Tom had very little experience with mental illness. His attitude toward his stepdaughter was getting worse. He thought Shannon was using us to get out of raising her child. More than once I found myself in the middle, trying to diffuse an argument between the two people I loved as Tom's frustration with his lazy stepdaughter increased.

One day in late spring, 2006, she was outside with Martin, who was now thirteen months old and learning to walk. I was cleaning the kitchen but kept glancing out the window to check on them. Martin suddenly tripped and fell face-first into a mud puddle. She didn't notice. I watched in horror from the kitchen window as Martin began choking on the mud. He was struggling to get up, and couldn't. Bolting for the front door, I leaped down five stairs and pulled the choking baby out of the puddle.

"What the hell is wrong with you? He could have drowned!" I yelled while scooping the mud out of his mouth. "You have to pay attention to him when he's outside. My God, Shannon, he could've died!" I shouted.

She grabbed another cigarette and walked away.

You're a lousy mother. You almost killed him again. You're stupid. Did you think you could take care of him? You are a worthless piece of shit!

Adding to our irritation was the additional cost of caring for Martin and Shannon. We found daycare for Martin immediately after the mud puddle incident. Although money wasn't the main issue, we were now caring for Shannon and Martin, paying for all their medical bills and food, which added to the tension in the house.

We carefully monitored Shannon's alone time with Martin. Tom would return home from work about an hour earlier than me. Shannon would then retrieve Martin from daycare. It was a quick 10-minute round-trip.

Shannon's behavior continued to get worse. Whenever I would ask her to help with anything, she would stare at me, her eyes filled with hate. "You were a bitch as a mother. You made me do all the housework when you were at your job. I had to cook all the meals. You never made the boys do anything." She would stare at both Tom and me with eyes that can only be described as evil. "I hate you. I hate you both. My father is much better than you."

My answer was usually the same: "You smoke too much. It's making you agitated. You've got to quit." Then I would count her pills in her Paxil bottle to make sure she was taking them as prescribed.

Often the pill count was incorrect. So I started making her take them in front of me, checking her mouth to make sure she swallowed them. There were also days when she would refuse. "Take your meds, or get out of this house !" I would yell.

"You can't force me to take these. You both get joy out of torturing me. Go to hell!"

After one such episode of her verbal abuse, Tom snapped. He pushed Shannon up against the kitchen cabinet and told her to move out. "I go to work every day. I pay the bills around here. You won't do anything around here. The least you can do is show your mother and me some respect!" he yelled.

She melted into a pile of weeping fury, at the same time shaking, terrified. I ran over to protect my daughter.

"You get the hell out of this house!" I screamed at Tom. "What the fuck are you doing to my child?"

I, too, was yelling and weeping and crying. Even as I screamed at him, I knew that I wanted to do the same thing to her. I wanted her out of the house and out of our lives. But what would happen to Martin then? Shannon pushed me aside and ran up to her room.

As the days passed, Shannon smoked more and more. It was like having a smokestack for a daughter. Cigarette butts were everywhere: in her car, in the barn, on the back stairs. Tom and I tried hiding her smokes, attempting to limit her smoking to one pack a day. But she would scrounge around the house, often stealing any money she could find so she could buy more. My marriage was falling apart. And her life had become like the cigarette ashes on the lawn.

7

I knew Shannon needed to be in the hospital. But I knew from working in the psychiatric wards that unless an adult was suicidal or homicidal, there wasn't much anyone could do. Repeatedly, I begged her to go to the hospital. Again and again, she refused.

Then one day in late June, when I got home from work, Shannon was sitting on the back stairs sobbing. "I think I'm going to die. If I stay here, I'm going to hurt you." The sobbing was nothing new, but the next words that came out of her mouth felt like the cold blade of a knife penetrating deep into my soul. Martin was just fourteen months old at the time.

"I can't live like this anymore. I just want to die! I hate Martin and you and Tom. I hate my life. I'm a horrible mother. I should never have had him. I want him to die."

"Depression," we said and drove her to a local hospital in Erie, Pennsylvania. She stayed there for two weeks. We would bring baby Martin to see her—only through the glass door. She couldn't hold him; she couldn't kiss him. He was little. How could she have ever tried to hurt him? Why didn't she want him? What made her so evil? Of course, we had all heard about post-partum depression, and we were pretty sure that was the problem. At first we were told that Shannon probably just needed to start taking her anti-depressants. Again, we felt relief.

We still had not realized the scope of her illness. Upon reading her discharge papers, we became aware the new diagnoses. It wasn't just depression. According to her psychiatrist, Shannon had bipolar disorder, major depressive disorder, obsessive-compulsive disorder and body dysmorphia (an illness in which she saw herself as deformed). We didn't want to believe it.

Before she was released, her counselors signed her up for an outpatient mental health program at the hospital. For six weeks she drove there every weekday. To support Shannon, I took a leave of absence from work so I could be home to take care of her and Martin.

Tom struggled with the knowledge that Shannon was indeed very ill. He had been certain she was faking it. For a while, he withdrew and avoided Shannon. The psychiatrist changed her medications many times over those six weeks, trying to find the right combination that would stop the anger, the self-loathing, and the depression. The medications made her gain weight.

You're ugly; you're fat. You have fake boobs. Everybody hates you.

After six weeks I went back to work and Martin went back to daycare. We had decided we couldn't leave Martin alone with Shannon at all. Every day, I'd drive him to daycare before I went to work. Then Tom would pick him up when he'd finished his workday. We were concerned that if she were left alone with Martin, even for a few minutes, he would get hurt. We didn't believe that she would intentionally hurt him, just that she wasn't capable of keeping an active toddler safe.

Then one day in 2007, when Martin was just two years old, she looked in the mirror and realized she was so ugly that no one would ever like her. Her head was oddly shaped, her chest sunken in, her clothes didn't fit. She emptied her closets and her drawers as she kept trying on different outfits. Soon there was a huge pile of clothes flung all over the room like used tissues. She carried them outside and burned them in the fire pit. Finding some of her brothers' old clothes she put them on to cover up the ugliness. She shaved her head. Completely bald, she shaved off her eyebrows, too, and then painted fake eyebrows above her eyes.

Tom and I were stunned when we came home from work. "What did you do to yourself? What is wrong with you?" I yelled. Martin looked a little confused when he came home from daycare, but then held out his arms to her.

She wouldn't shower. She smoked more and more, first one pack a day, then two, then three, then four. Soon she was smoking all day. That was all. That was her life.

One day I asked her to sweep the kitchen floor, and she wouldn't answer, just sat in a chair and stared at the floor. Something inside of me snapped. I crumpled up sections of the newspaper and started throwing them at her.

"What have you done around here all day?" I yelled. "I took your child to daycare, worked all day, and then Tom picked him up. You haven't done a damn thing around here." I pushed her off the chair.

She just gazed at me with a blank expression on her face. Then Martin started throwing the newspaper at her, too. I was horrified. How could I have let my emotions get so out of control? I ran over to her and hugged her. There was no response.

8

When Shannon finally started seeing a psychiatrist and a counselor regularly, she began to change. Week by week, month by month, she started to interact again with her son in small ways. She began reading him stories at night. Then she started to help around the house. She baked cookies again. There were days when she seemed almost normal. There was hope in her eyes, as *they* stopped telling her that she was ugly, stopped telling her to hurt her child, and stopped telling her to burn things. She slowed down the pace of her cigarette smoking.

We still kept the now-toddler in daycare, though, believing that he was safer there. She would hold him and cuddle him at night. Many nights she and he would fall asleep in the rocking chair together.

He was an active baby, and as all babies sometimes try to do, he would attempt to hit her when he didn't want to take a nap or eat his peas. Most mothers know that babies sometimes have temper tantrums. But she would often hear a whisper.

He hates you.

For the next year and a half, she lived with us. Occasionally it would be fun. Sometimes it was not. She became what we called manipulative. She was on medication, so there was no excuse for her behavior, we thought. She seemed to enjoy being a mother, though. Playing with Martin made her smile and laugh.

At times, we lived with fear: fear that she would get worse and fear that Eric would find out how sick she was and try to get custody of Martin.

When Martin was three and a half, Shannon began seeing a new psychiatrist. For five months in the winter of 2008 and the spring of 2009, she became that daughter that we had once loved and the mother that Martin needed. She would often tell me that she fought so hard to get well because of her love for that little boy. He had come into her life to save her, she said.

Because Shannon was doing so well, in the spring of 2009, when Martin had just turned four, we started leaving him home alone with Shannon. She seemed to genuinely love Martin, taking him for walks to the creek and driving him to local playgrounds. She kept him clean, cooked him meals, and played games with him on the floor.

9

Every other weekend, Martin's dad had visitation rights. They were court-ordered supervised visits because of Eric's inability to care for a child by himself. After meeting Eric's new girlfriend, Hope, we felt that Martin would be safe with her. Hope had a son who was a few years older than Martin, and they played together. Because she had an apartment, we would drop Martin off there to play.

When Eric's girlfriend became pregnant, she found out that Eric was not the nice tall, handsome man she had thought he was. Just like Eric did to Shannon, he started calling Hope names and refused to help around the house.

Hope stayed with Eric until shortly after the birth of their daughter. He began smoking around his newborn, who contracted pneumonia. He began staying out late, drinking and gambling. He stopped taking his medication. She soon realized that Eric was sick. His behavior was affecting her child and her health. It didn't take her long to throw Eric out of her apartment. He called the police, telling them that Hope was an unfit mother.

Because of the court order stating that Eric needed someone to supervise the visits, Shannon applied to the family court for a hearing to appoint a new supervisor.

At the hearing, she and Eric agreed to have Eric's father, 'Papa,' supervise the visits. We contacted Hope, who was now the mother of Eric's daughter, to coordinate the court orders.

Martin and his new baby half-sister began to go to Papa's apartment in Erie, Pennsylvania, every other Saturday to play and visit with their father. Eric's ex-girlfriend, Hope, also attended the visits, as she refused to leave her baby, who was still breastfeeding.

It might have been ok. Maybe Shannon would have continued to get better. But one day, Eric's girlfriend couldn't go to the visitation, so I dropped both Martin and his baby sister off at Papa's apartment. When I went to pick him up, just four hours later, I immediately knew that something was wrong. Papa wouldn't look at me when I entered the apartment. Eric was lying on the couch. I assumed he was sleeping off another alcohol- and drug-induced coma. Martin had been crying and ran over to hug me. I loaded Martin's half-sister in the car, then dropped her off at Hope's house.

Martin clung to me when we got home and was quieter than usual. At first, when I asked him what was wrong, he told me that he had been bad and Papa had made him stand in the corner. Exhausted, he fell asleep on the couch. Not wanting to wake him, I left him in his clothes and put him in his bed.

The next morning was a beautiful summer day. We all put on our bathing suits after lunch and headed out to the pool. Martin kept pulling at his bathing suit as if it was uncomfortable.

"What's the matter, Martin? Is your bathing suit too tight?" I asked him.

His answer would change all of our lives forever and would send Shannon into a freefall from which we were not sure she would ever recover.

Little Martin's answer was "Papa put his finger in my butt." No. I didn't believe him. I asked him again, this time in front of Shannon and Tom. He repeated his answer. Shannon collapsed on the floor. Tom immediately stated he was going to kill Papa and headed for the stairs.

"Where are you going?" I asked Tom.

"Up to get my shotgun. I'm going to kill that son-of-a-bitch!" he snarled.

"That's not going to fix anything. You'll just go to jail," I shouted.

As a registered nurse, I had worked in an emergency room. I should have known what to do. But at that moment, I couldn't think or act. I was no longer a nurse, but a grandmother, disgusted and numb at the same time. I asked Tom what we should do.

The visit to the emergency room, the call to the police station, the examination by the forensic nurse, and the many court hearings that followed were too much for Shannon's fragile mental state. The one thing she had come to love, the one reason she had tried to get well, had been hurt. It was her fault.

You didn't protect him. You sent him to that place. You are responsible. You are ugly. You will never be a good mother. You tried to kill him. YOU hurt him. You molested him, not somebody else. You need to go to jail, forever.

Martin met with the police, the district attorney, his physician, and counselors. He described the color of the couch and where each person had been in the house when the incident took place. He described how it felt. He never wavered from his story.

We couldn't believe that the state of Pennsylvania would put a four-year-old on the witness stand. He had told his story over and over to many people and had even been videotaped by the district attorney's office.

"The accused has the right to face his accuser," the DA told us.

"But he's only four," I replied. "Don't tell me that Papa's lawyer will cross-examine him! That's insane!"

During the trial, in December, 2009, Papa's lawyer tried to get Martin to change his story. "No, I told the truth," he said.

During the trial, when she was on the witness stand, Shannon could hardly speak. When asked a question, as the minutes ticked by she stared at the floor without an answer. "I just wanted him to be safe," she finally sobbed.

Tom also cried during that trial. Martin had changed, Tom said on the witness stand. Martin wouldn't let anybody hold him except Grandma and Mommy. He was afraid to go to the bathroom, afraid of the dark. He wouldn't take his clothes off for baths. He had night terrors.

The jury deliberated for seven hours; the trial ended with a hung jury. Of the twelve jurors, only one man didn't believe the little four-year-old on the witness stand, playing with the microphone. The District Attorney wanted to go forward with another trial, and we agreed. As we prepared for that, winter turned into spring. Shannon was mostly uncommunicative. When she did speak, it was of self-hatred, and of death.

Martin was five years old by then. Shannon once again spent her days chain-smoking. Angry during the daytime, she spent her nights crying. She would refuse all the medications that had previously helped her. When we forced her to take them we would all argue and yell at each other. We even threatened to throw her out of the house if she didn't take them, and after a while she would swallow the pills.

Then, out of the blue, she began telling us bizarre sexual stories. "My brothers used to make me undress at parties. Their friends all groped me."

"One night an alien came into my bedroom and tried to molest me."

"I'm messed up because my father sexually abused me."

"I can't hug you anymore, Mom, because I'm sexually attracted to you."

One night after I went to bed, she began stroking Tom's leg. Stunned, he hurried out of the room. After that, he didn't feel comfortable being left alone with her. We never knew if what she said was a lie or the truth. We didn't understand that she was unable to tell the difference between the two.

Then in May, a month after Martin turned five, Shannon called up the district attorney's office and told them she had molested her son.

 10

When I returned home from work that day, I found two Child Protective Services (CPS) workers in my driveway. They informed me that they were going to put Martin in foster care unless Shannon moved out of the house immediately.

Later that day, the police came to the house and questioned Martin without Shannon present. He wouldn't get off my lap during the questioning, and denied any abuse by his mother.

We were terrified. By this time, no other family member would let our daughter, this disturbed person, move in with them, as all had been subject to her verbal abuse. None of her brothers felt comfortable around her anymore. She did not want to move in with her father. After all the accusations she had thrown at him, he didn't encourage her to do that, either.

While Tom and I filled out the initial paperwork to become temporary foster parents for our grandson, Shannon drove herself to a hospital in upstate New York.

Our house needed to be inspected, CPS told us. Our well needed to be tested. We signed papers agreeing that we would never leave Martin alone with his mother.

At the same time, we realized there would not be another trial. We knew that Shannon had not hurt her son, but who would believe her or us after her report to the DA? And Shannon was far too fragile to go through another trial. We called up the assistant district attorney and told her we were not going forward with the retrial. Not wanting Papa to get away unencumbered, the DA convinced Papa and his attorney to sign a statement saying he would never again have contact with Martin. Papa readily agreed.

Once again Shannon was admitted to a mental health hospital. The decision to go to a hospital in New York rather than one in Pennsylvania was the best decision Shannon could have made. The State of New York had an amazing program for both the mentally ill and the disabled. After another two weeks in the hospital, Shannon applied to a group home where other mentally ill individuals were also housed. We had been unaware that such a place existed.

While Tom and I went through the process of becoming temporary foster parents, Shannon started the process of being discharged to a group home for the mentally ill. Martin was given a child advocacy attorney, and we hired an attorney for ourselves. Because Martin was legally considered to be in foster care, CPS workers were also involved. Tom and I both signed up for an eight-week course to become foster parents as we filed for permanent custody of Martin.

Of course, there were many court hearings. Eric decided that he didn't want us to raise his son, and attempted to get custody of Martin. We requested that Eric have drug testing completed. Martin's attorney, as well as the CPS workers, asked Eric and anyone living with Eric to submit to background checks.

Of course, Eric refused both. He had been arrested in the past for assault. His younger brother, a convicted felon, who lived with him, had recently been arrested for endangering the welfare of minors. His older brother, who also lived in Eric's house, had also just been arrested, for breaking his girlfriend's arm. We learned that the FBI had confiscated the home computer earlier in the year and had found child pornography on it. Eric also told Shannon he would not keep his father, Papa, from visiting with Martin, even though Papa had already signed the paperwork.

The judge advised Eric that he could see Martin only at a neutral place that would provide supervised visitation, as none of his family was deemed to be appropriate to provide the visitation. Eric, thinking that he could obtain custody of Martin once CPS was no longer involved, agreed that Tom and I could have custody of Martin.

I remember tears rolling down my face when the judge read the order. I did not know how our attorney possibly could have achieved the miracle. Eric's only contact with Martin would be in bi-weekly phone calls. I was unaware that after the hearing, Eric immediately walked out of the courtroom and down the hall, and filed an appeal for custody of Martin.

In the court paperwork that arrived within the week, Eric stated that we were unfit parents who had allowed his son to be molested by our daughter, his ex-girlfriend. He made bizarre remarks about our being friends with his ex-girlfriend, and my molesting his daughter. He had a video of a wailing baby Martin at the age of eight months, crawling on the floor while Shannon tried to knock the infant over. Eric failed to realize that because he had taken the video, he was also guilty; he could be heard in the background laughing while baby Martin was crying.

In the first hearing in which Eric attempted to get custody, our attorney explained to the judge that Eric had filed the paperwork immediately after he'd signed the first custody agreement. In fact, it was the same day.

"Why did you do that?" the judge asked Eric.

His response was "You people were making it too hard for me to see my son."

"You had your chance the day you agreed to the last court order." The judge was angry and threw out the appeal.

That did not stop Eric. He filed new paperwork right after that hearing, stating that because we thought we were good grandparents, those thoughts proved we were insane. The judge dismissed that appeal.

For a third time, Eric filed for custody. Finally, the judge, tiring of Eric's antics, had him removed from the courtroom. Two sheriffs escorted him out of the courthouse. The judge advised him not to come back, or he would risk jail time.

The lawyer's fees cost us thousands of dollars. Eric, of course, spent no money on the appeals.

11

In the meantime, Shannon had moved into the group home. There she was expected to contribute to the house by completing assigned chores, cooking meals, and keeping her room clean. Shannon was also expected to attend classes to learn about her illness. She was warned that no alcohol or non-prescribed drugs were allowed in the house. Each day she took her medications in front of a staff member.

It was after that hospitalization that we first saw the discharge paperwork with the dreaded diagnosis: schizophrenia. And for the first time, we realized that "they" were the voices. "They" were not the people standing in line or the students whispering. They were in Shannon's body and brain, possessing every part of her being and soul.

It was difficult for Martin, who was five years old by then, to have his mother move out of our house. Although he had been living with us since he he'd been a year old, he loved his mother and had seemed to be very accepting of her illness. We explained to him that Mommy was sick and trying to get better. We told him when Mommy was well she would be coming back home. We honestly believed that, in spite of the illness, Shannon would one day be well enough to take over the full-time role of being Martin's mother.

We took Martin to visit his mother every weekend. She seemed genuinely happy to see him, often crying when he arrived. But usually after 20 minutes, she had had enough and drifted mindlessly off to some unknown region of her psyche. "You can go now," she would tell us.

She would sometimes tell me things about the other residents. "An ambulance came last night and took Justin away."

"Why? What happened?" I asked.

"He's dead. They say he killed himself." She said it like she was talking about what she'd had for dinner. There was a chilling lack of emotion.

On another occasion, she told me about Sarah. "She cuts herself. Last night she cut up her face and went to the hospital."

"That's terrible," I said. "Why do people do that?"

She answered, "The pain inside hurts so much that it is a relief to feel the pain outside."

"Do you cut yourself?" I asked.

"No. Not yet. But sometimes I want to."

Martin was in first grade by then and had significant behavioral problems in school. He constantly poked other children in the arm and had what he called "meltdowns." We had taken him to counseling, right after the incident with Papa; now Martin started counseling again. We lived with the knowledge that mental illness is often inherited. Did our little grandson have any chance of growing up to be a normal human being?

Shannon's father and stepmother wanted to help us with raising Martin. Every other weekend they brought Martin to their house, sometimes just for a day, sometimes for the weekend. Martin loved the visits with his grandpa. And we were grateful for the break.

 12

Shannon was living in the group home. She was taking her medications and seemed to be slowly improving. Her medications frequently changed, as Shannon told her psychiatrist that the side-effects were unbearable. At times she would hide the medications in her mouth and spit them out in the toilet instead of taking them.

At night she would leave the group home and go to a local playground, cleaning up trash that older children had left. She said she was trying to make up for being a lousy mother. Shannon seemed to be unaware that the behavior of going out alone at night as a young woman could be risky.

Once in a while, she would stay overnight at a male friend's apartment. Some days she would dress like a hooker. On other days, her voice would get low and she would dress and act like a man. On rare occasions, she would dress in clothes that we thought were normal.

The staff at the house became more and more worried about her actions. They believed she needed to go back to the hospital to change medications, but she would refuse, and they were unable to force her. The law stated that if she became a threat to herself or others, she could be committed for a few days. If she did not pose a threat, there was nothing anyone could do.

I continued to pray, to ask God for a miracle to save my daughter. I asked for a cure; I begged for help. Often I cried myself to sleep. What had happened to my child?

Where was that little girl who played tricks on us and who danced on the porch in the sunlight? Where was the happy teenager who teased the truckers? Where was my daughter hiding? Why couldn't she be normal, have a job, have a life, and care for her child? By this time, Shannon was unable to perform simple math problems. My beautiful daughter, who had made the Dean's list in college, could barely read. I knew she was only a shadow of her former self.

 13

"Did you say my butt was too big? I heard you say that."

At the time, Martin and I were walking with Shannon from the group home to a playground.

"He hates me. Martin, you hate Mommy, don't you? You know I'm not a girl. I can't possibly be your mother."

Martin looked confused.

"Shannon, please don't tell Martin that. It upsets him."

"You know it's the truth. You know you said that to me. Stop lying to me! Get out of here and don't come back. I don't need your lies or you. Just let me die."

That day, I called Shannon's counselors and told them Shannon wanted to kill herself. It wasn't exactly the truth, but I was desperate to have her hospitalized. Her behavior was reckless; she was "accidentally" cutting herself while shaving her legs. Every phone call from her was frightening. Martin had learned to hand me the phone when she called. "Grandma, she's talking crazy again." He didn't want to hear her confused words.

She was hospitalized again. Tom and I, as well as Shannon's father, were all taking more active roles in her recovery. Attending psychiatric appointments with her, I saw how easily she had convinced the counselors and physicians that she wasn't having any symptoms. She would deny she heard voices and deny she had spit out her medications. She didn't trust anyone enough to tell them the truth.

I spent countless hours researching mental illness and speaking with many professionals who worked in the field of psychiatry. I went to the hospital and the group home and spoke with her counselors and her social workers. One of my friends, Bob, a psychiatric nurse who was working at Warren State Mental Institution, said that maybe Shannon was having seizures. He had seen seizures cause bizarre behaviors. I offered that theory to her psychiatrist, who listened but didn't agree with that theory. Again, Shannon's medications changed.

This time, when Shannon was released, I knew exactly what medications she was on and how they were affecting her behavior. As Shannon became a little more rational, once again Tom and I began to have hope.

In 2012, after more than two years in the group home, Shannon decided she was well enough to move into an apartment. She had been participating in her programs, taking her medications, and caring for the gardens around the residence. Although she didn't want to spend much time with Martin, she started to make friends with the people in her classes. We thought the move might be good for, her as Shannon was not getting along with her roommate in the group home. We felt as if she had progressed far enough in the group home that getting an apartment would improve her mental health.

Her counselors said it was a "supported" apartment. They would still be checking in on her and helping her with the activities of daily living. They would help her set up her pill boxes so she would be taking the correct medications. And they would meet with her regularly. They would arrange transportation to the grocery store, Walmart, the laundromat, and doctor's appointments. Shannon was expected to keep the apartment neat and continue to attend her mental health programs.

She seemed to enjoy her apartment. She kept it neat. Although the supported apartment lease stated that no pets were allowed, we bribed the landlord with a $500 deposit so she could get a cat. She had always loved animals, and we felt that a cat would ease the loneliness of living alone. She was like a seed that had been planted, and that seed was beginning to sprout.

That newfound growth didn't last more than a few months. "Shannon, did you eat anything today?" I asked her on one visit. There was little food in the refrigerator, or in the kitchen cabinets. A stack of dirty dishes was in the sink.

I had noticed a pair of men's work boots in her doorway. From the bedroom came a new voice. A man in his fifties entered the room. Sam was large and overweight. He smelled as if he hadn't bathed in several weeks. His clothes were dirty, and he had no teeth. He had been living in a cabin in the woods with no heat.

"I met him downtown a few weeks ago. I felt sorry for him," Shannon explained to me. "So I said he could live with me until it got warmer in the spring."

I took Shannon out shopping for food that afternoon. "Do you think having Sam live with you is a good idea?" I asked her.

"It's my life, Mom, stay out of it."

She seemed genuinely happy to get groceries, filling up the shopping cart with over $200 worth of them. As we were driving back to the apartment, she started getting extremely agitated. Her voice lowered into a man's.

"Why are you talking like a man?"

"I am a man, and you know it," she answered. "Why do you keep trying to turn me into something I am not? You know I look like a man. Why do you keep lying to me?"

You are a man. Sam doesn't like you. He likes your mother. Sam wants to sleep with your mother. He thinks she's cuter than you. He knows her breasts are real. Your mother slept with him already.

I helped Shannon carry the groceries into her apartment. I started to help her unpack the bags when she turned to me and yelled, "You take everything from me! First you took my son, and now you're sleeping with my man. I hate you! Don't you ever come back here!"

Why did Shannon hate me? I didn't know what I could have done. I thought I had been trying so hard to accept her and her illness. The voices must be back, I thought. But how could they be back again? Trying to keep the tears from streaming down my face, I left her apartment.

The next several months were heartbreaking. Shannon did not want to see her son. She wouldn't answer the phone when I called. When I tried to visit her, she wouldn't answer the door. Again, she started drinking alcohol and using street drugs. She stopped shopping for food and again stopped taking her medication.

One day, as I was in the car, parked on the street outside her apartment, I saw that she had thrown out her furniture, and large trash bags filled with her clothes were in the dumpster. I banged on her door and demanded to be let in.

When she finally opened the door, what I saw scared me. The apartment, which had been so clean, was littered with trash. Shannon had lost a lot of weight and looked like a skeleton. Her clothes, which throughout the illness had been clean, were filthy. The cat hadn't been fed for a while, and ran up to me, hungry for some food.

"The cat is evil," she said. "She stares at me and wants to kill me."

Don't let your mother touch you. She wants to be your lover. She knows you're a man. She knows you want to molest her. She wants you to die. She has a stepdaughter who is so pretty. And you are so ugly.

"Oh, honey," I said as I tried to hug her.

"Don't touch me. Don't come near me. They all tell me you want me to die."

I saw Shannon's medications strewn about in her kitchen.

When I left, I immediately called Shannon's counselors. "Something's wrong. I don't think she's taking her medications anymore. She's very thin; I know she's not eating right. When was the last time a counselor visited her? Someone must have seen these changes."

They assured me they would visit Shannon the next day.

"Shannon's refusing to go back to the hospital," her counselor told me over the phone the following day. "We can't force her, you know."

14

As Shannon's condition continued to deteriorate, we began receiving weird text messages from her. The following are excerpts from the messages we received over several days in February, 2013.

Feb 11

"You cheated on me because you cheated on my father. You chose Tom over my Dad? My dad was way-way more handsome than Tom. And then of all people Tom who used you for your money and constantly made you jealous?"

Feb 12th 12:00 AM

"I hid my identity for years and years, and you conned me into living a god damned lie. You only loved George!!! You never let me be one of the boys; you both told me that I had to love my brothers. You tricked me into thinking that I was a beautiful woman, and all the other girls would be jealous. You lied and covered up and lied and lied. My kid hates me, and he loves you. No, he does not love you."

Feb 12th 12:21 AM

"You know I was a jealous motherfucker and conned me into all of it. You knew I was troubled. And you knew how to make me feel insignificant compared to the rest of my brothers. Your family liked Olivia, and they hated me."

Feb 12th 12:31 AM

"You all got joy out of making me feel insignificant, ugly worthless and a hater of myself and my bloodline. Breastless masculine should I believe there is a God or a higher power. Life did not happen at all Rosy for me. Stop calling me Rosy. Stop comparing me to Rosy."

Feb 12th 12:47 AM

"Control freaks, seducers."

Feb 11th 4:41 PM

"I am sorry for being inappropriate and vile towards family members, and I understand that I have been shunned and judged for my actions. I'm sorry for pissing everyone off. I am a lamo with fake boobs who violates people. I struggle with jealousy. Sorry for being offensive. I don't want to be attracted to my brothers or sisters. I dislike straight people, so I molest them. Bye."

At first, I tried to ignore the texts. What was I supposed to do? Then as Shannon started sending them out to my sisters and brothers, and to her father, and to Tom, and to my aunts and uncles, I knew I had to respond.

I tried to call her, but she wouldn't answer her cell phone, and she had turned off the answering machine on her apartment phone.

I sent her texts. "Please take your meds. Or go to the hospital. I'm worried about you. Stop texting my sister!"

Her response was, "Sorry I molested Tom. I'm sorry I kept staring at his privates."

Again I sent Shannon a text message, "Take your meds."

This time, she sent a text to Tom. "Like I said sorry for staring at your privates and at mom's boobs...she's not my wife and I'm sorry in some fucked up way dilapidated way that I got jealous of my mom because her boobs are real and mine are not. It's difficult to accept that I turned out this way."

Feb 12th 6:36 AM

"I violate babies I can't be trusted. I am a manly jealous gay. I violated everyone. Manly jealous loser. No one likes me. I should have never given birth. I'm an unfit mother. I can't tell the difference between truth and a lie. I'm scared to die. I'm afraid of getting killed. I'm afraid they will kill me. Please don't kill me. I'm a criminal abuser."

This time, I responded more forcefully, "Stop texting people. Stop texting your Dad! You are not an abuser. You are not a man!! Stop smoking, take your meds, go to your classes or I will turn off your phone."

Shannon's texts didn't stop.

"Scared Scared Scared Scared of my sister Scared of my brothers. I don't know if I'm a man or a woman. I am not pretty. My baby never liked me. Boys don't like me. Girls don't like me. No one has ever liked me. I'm a failure of the human race. I have no dignity. There is no hope. I give up. There is no future for me. I don't understand what normal is. I'm a freak. Why would my son like me? My baby's face is mutilated. I'm not sure that I'm even human. What I did was inhuman."

At 8 AM, I turned off the data for Shannon's phone. She could still call people, but she couldn't text anyone.

At 3 PM, I received a phone message from Shannon. "All is well. Please turn my phone back on."

At 7 PM, I received another voice message. "I'm fine. How is everyone over there? Please turn my phone back on."

I called Shannon back. "Shannon," I said, "You need to go to the hospital. Your voices are back; you are very ill. I'm worried about you. You're dressing like a man again. You're not a man; you're a beautiful woman."

"I'm fine."

 15

Several hours later, on February 13th at 3 AM, I received a phone call.

"Hello?"

"Hello, this is the police."

"Yes?" I thought I was going to vomit.

"I have your daughter, Shannon, here. She says she killed her son."

"That's not possible," I said. "He lives with my husband and me. He hasn't seen his mother in months. She's mentally ill. She needs to be in the hospital."

"She says there's blood all over her apartment. And she says people are trying to kill her," the officer responded.

"Please take her to the hospital. She's on disability for mental illness."

For the fourth time, Shannon was admitted to the mental health unit of the hospital.

This time was the worst. Shannon was not only hearing voices but seeing bizarre, violent things. She told her counselor that there was blood all over the bathroom, from where she had slaughtered her child. There were bugs and snakes all over the walls, she said. Along with hearing and seeing things, she smelled odors that did not exist; she thought her bed was on fire. She said she had been raped.

This time, no medications seemed to stop the voices and images. The physicians kept Shannon sedated, which seemed to help a little, although she slept twenty hours out of each day. After two weeks, she was once again released to her apartment. That lasted less than two days. She again went to the police station, telling the officer that she should be arrested and jailed. Shannon was re-admitted to the hospital.

When I went to visit her in the hospital the following day, I thought I was looking at a dead person. Shannon's skin was sallow. Her eyes were hollow. She didn't answer any of my questions, just cried and cried. When I tried to hug her, there was no response.

When I got home after that visit, there was a police car in the driveway. "Your daughter called 911 and told us you were abusing her son."

Tom and Martin had been home when the officer had first arrived. They were enjoying "boys' night out," a ritual they often practiced when I was not home. It consisted of the two boys sitting together, eating popcorn and watching movies.

We explained to the officer that Shannon was very ill. After learning that Shannon was in the mental health section of the hospital, the officer started to relax. He spoke with Martin, who had wandered off to play games in the back room. Satisfied that all was well, he left. I called the hospital and asked them to try to keep Shannon away from the phones. They said they would try.

Another week went by, with little change in Shannon's condition.

"She's a tortured soul," her social worker told me. "She is very scared, and nothing seems to help. She seems to hate herself. We don't seem to be able to help her here. We don't think she can go back to the group home. I'm afraid we're going to have to commit her to a mental health institution."

That night we all cried. Shannon cried because she hated herself and wanted to die. We cried because our beautiful daughter was lost in a hell that we could not comprehend. She was gone. Our daughter had slowly died a little at a time from this horrible illness. I prayed that she would pass away as I could not bear to see Shannon suffering. I had been a hospice nurse. I had heard many of my patients' families repeatedly say that their loved one's death was a relief for them. I knew all too well what that meant. But how does a mother give up on a child? How could God let my daughter suffer so much? How could we all go on with our lives, knowing that Shannon would spend the rest of her life in an institution—not just in an institution but also living with such self-loathing and agony?

It reminded me of a day twenty years ago when my five-year-old nephew had died during open heart surgery. Just like that day, I felt a pain so deep in my soul that even the simple act of breathing hurt.

I did not know it at the time, but that day marked a turning point in my understanding of mental illness. The illness could have taken Shannon then; she could have given up. I knew that many people had chosen the easy way out and committed suicide. I knew that death would have ended her suffering.

But this is not the end of the story. Shannon did not give up, neither did her psychiatrist, or her counselors, or her family. The rest of this story is the story of a strong woman who loved her son and her family enough to fight her way out of hell. It is a story of a family who accepted a daughter with a mental illness, and who stopped crying over the pain of wanting things to be "normal." We would all soon learn the meaning of inner strength.

 16

We met with the social worker at the hospital. Tom and I brought along the notes we had been keeping about Shannon's different medications; we had some ideas about which ones had worked and which ones had seemed to make her worse.

"I know there are injectable medications, rather than oral medications," I said. "Every time Shannon seems to be getting better, we think the voices tell her to stop taking her meds. We know that Risperdal (an anti-psychotic) has helped her in the past. The anti-depressant she is on right now seems to have made her worse. She responded fairly well to Paxil in the past."

We handed the social worker the list of the medications with the symptoms we had noted.

One of the disturbing facts about people with mental illness is that many don't take their medications. Is it the voices telling them to stop? Is it the fact that most of the medications have unpleasant side effects? Is it that the mentally ill person just forgets? Or is it for different reasons?

We knew about one injection, Clozaril. Our nurse friend, Bob, had told us that it seemed to help many people with schizophrenia. But we also knew that Shannon would have to have blood work completed on a regular basis, and her past non-compliance made that an issue. Clozaril was also very expensive, costing over $1000 a month, and probably wouldn't be approved by Shannon's insurance.

The doctors came up with a plan. Risperdal was now available as a bi-monthly injection. Shannon would still have to take oral Risperdal, too, along with other antipsychotics, sleep medications, sedatives, antidepressants, and medications to combat the side effects of the other medications. They also listened to our ideas about seizures causing some of the symptoms. Although an EEG that might have shown seizure activity was inconclusive, her psychiatrist placed her on the medication Klonopin. A tranquilizer, Klonopin was also used to combat seizure activity. After another week in the hospital, she showed some improvement; Shannon was discharged to a different group home.

 17

The new group home seemed like a better fit for Shannon. She had a room to herself on the second floor. Ten other people with mental illness also lived in the house. Each three-room area had a lounge and a bathroom. The main living space had a huge kitchen and dining room. There was an outdoor porch. A washer and dryer were on the first floor.

Again, Shannon was expected to attend classes, to complete household chores, and to take her medications. By this time, she was on eight different medications, as well as her bi-monthly injections. She continued to smoke cigarettes that caused her to cough constantly, and her history of poor oral hygiene caused her teeth to decay.

Shannon had known one of the counselors from the previous group home in which she had lived. That counselor became a lifeline for Shannon and us. The house manager was smart and reliable. We felt we could call him anytime and he would listen to our concerns.

At first, we were unsure if any of these changes would help this very ill person who had once been our daughter. We had to make some decisions about what was best for Shannon, as well as her son, and what was best for us.

Any person's mental illness affects everyone surrounding that person. First, Tom and I and Shannon's father had to stop being hurt every time Shannon called us names. We had to stop commenting every time Shannon cut her hair or her eyebrows. We all had to stop commenting on what she wore or how she looked. We had to love her exactly the way she was.

We, the members of her family, including Martin, had to recognize the signs of relapse and immediately tell her counselors about those signs. We had to continue to tell Shannon every day that we loved her. And we had to have good communication with the group home manager and physicians.

I stopped asking God to make my child normal. Instead, I prayed for her to be happy, and asked for guidance for all of us. And I had to let go of my daughter. I had to believe that she was on her journey. I used to tell Tom that the saddest thing in my life was the fact that my daughter was so ill. I had to learn to be happy with whatever Shannon was or would become, and not only accept the changes but accept the illness.

Every time Shannon would take a few steps forward, she would take one backward. And those backward steps had to stop causing fear in all of us. I often wondered, if Shannon had been Tom's daughter, instead of mine, would I have stayed in our relationship? His love for me and his love for Shannon amazed me. Shannon's father, who had often been hurt by her accusations of his raping her or molesting her, also started to take a much more active role in her life. He started visiting her more, and calling her more frequently. He always told her he loved her.

A slow but steady healing began to take place. We as a family became closer. As we began to accept the illness, we began to accept our lives as good. We began to feel blessed: blessed that we lived in New York State, blessed that the group home was such a nice place, blessed that our daughter was alive.

Once day when I was putting Martin to bed, he started to cry. "I hate my life," he said. "I don't have a mother, and I don't have a father. I'm different from everyone else in my class."

"When Grandpa and I got married," I told Martin, "God knew that we were too old to have any more children, but that we wanted another child. So when you were up in heaven, he decided to let your mother give birth to you. He knew that you would end up being our child. And he knew that we would feel blessed to have you in our life. We love you as much as we love all of our children. You are very brave and very smart. Who knows, maybe one day, you might be the one to help cure your mother's illness."

The next day, Martin went into his class and informed his teacher that he was going to be a scientist. He explained that, like a when a computer had a virus, his mother's brain was "corrupt," and he was going to help save her.

 18

For the first few months after Shannon moved into the second group home, we would visit her frequently but stay only a few minutes. She seemed to get agitated when we stayed longer. We told her that she had to be honest with us and tell us when it was time for us to leave. She had to be able to tell us when we shouldn't visit her. As much as Tom wanted to see Shannon and hug her, he realized that Shannon might misinterpret his hugs so he would often stay home instead of visiting. I started asking Shannon permission to hug her, instead of just invading her private space.

Our visits became less frequent than they had in the past. Shannon didn't want to come to our house. She told us she felt like the voices were worse when she was there. She didn't want to visit her father. We slowly learned that we had to interpret many of Shannon's actions as her illness, and not as criticisms of us or our lives.

When she talked in the "man voice" and dressed like a man, we didn't react. In the past, I had asked her to stop. When she dressed up like a woman of the night, we didn't respond.

On one visit, Shannon asked me to take all of her "girl" clothes. "Just take them, Mom, I'm never going to look like a girl." Then she introduced me to her girlfriend, her lover.

"Nice to meet you," I responded as I shook her girlfriend's hand. The old me would have been horrified to see my beautiful daughter, now missing teeth, dressing like a man, and introducing me to her female lover. The new me was glad to see Shannon happy.

I took her clothes home with me and stored them in a closet. I was pretty sure that Shannon would want them back again at some point if she decided she wanted to look like a girl. And if not, the Salvation Army could always use more clothes.

Our commitment to constantly monitoring Shannon's medications began to pay off. I again attended psychiatric appointments with her and voiced concerns about her behaviors. As we began to see signs of hope, she began to feel hopeful. She started piano lessons and learned how to cook again. She started calling us more and calling her father. She would still occasionally forget her medications, but because the medication injections were long-lasting, the setbacks were temporary. It was as if she had been in an endless nightmare for nine years and was slowly starting to wake up.

 19

It was not a smooth trip out of hell for Shannon. One of the results of "awakening" was that Shannon was starting to grieve. She would cry over her confusion with math and reading, and she would cry over her lost teeth. The hardest thing to watch was when she would cry about Martin.

She had missed much of his life. He had turned nine after her last hospitalization. She hadn't been able to guide him in his life. She hadn't been able to be his mother, she said.

"You have to learn to forgive yourself for being ill," I told her. "Do people with brain tumors blame themselves for being sick? Or people with MS? You have an illness. You will probably be on medication for the rest of your life to help you cope with your illness. We are grateful that such medications exist."

"How can Martin ever love me, when I haven't been able to be his mother? How could he ever love me after the things I did to him?" she asked me.

"Martin is an amazing child. He loves you so much," I replied.

"How?" she asked.

"Because he only remembers the good parts. He talks about going to the creek with you. He remembers when you used to read him stories. The times you remember hurting him happened in your head. I don't think you ever actually hurt him," I said.

Martin was growing into an amazingly perceptive and compassionate child. As he started to accept his life circumstances, he also continued to experience more fear. Instead of feeling safer when Shannon started to get better, he was scared that he might have to leave our house and live with her. "Grandma, what if my mom wants me to live with her? I don't want to leave you and Grandpa."

And when I went on a trip out of town to care for a sick brother, he cried in school, worried that I wouldn't come back. "What if Grandma doesn't come back?" he asked Tom.

His counselor said he had abandonment issues. "Well, of course he does," Tom said. "Look at what he has lost. His grandfather molested him, his father is mentally ill and can't care for him, and his mother moved out of the house. He doesn't even know if she'll ever get better. All he has is us. And he's afraid of losing us, too."

He had been having nightmares ever since he'd been four years old. Martin's nightmares had been violent. He would tell me he was on a pirate ship where he was killed with a sword. He would describe the blood running down his arm and how it felt when he fell into the ocean. Other times he would dream that wolves were attacking him, and they were biting his face. He would wake up screaming, and I'd have to hold him until he fell asleep again. As difficult as it had been for us to accept our life, it was twice as hard for Martin.

The nightmares weren't going away. He was afraid to fall asleep. So Tom and I began a ritual every night of talking about what we were grateful for—in alphabetical order.

"Tonight we are grateful for food, Martin, you can start."

"Avocados."

"Beans," I said.

"Carrots," said Tom.

And on and on we would go, each night with a different subject, each night with new ideas. We completed that ritual every night for over six months. Over time, as Shannon started to get better, Martin started to get better, too. By the end of fourth grade, the nightmares were rare. He started to feel safe. We told him that his mother might never be able to live with him. She had an illness that would most likely be with her the rest of her life. He said he liked living with us.

We had always had animals in our house: dogs, cats, sometimes birds. Just before Martin's tenth birthday, when we rescued three feral kittens, Martin decided they were his. Caring for the tiny four-week-old kittens seemed to comfort him. One night the smallest kitten climbed on the couch and began trying to nurse on the blanket.

"She misses her mother," said Martin. As the tears welled up in his eyes, he continued, "Just like I miss mine."

"It's okay," I told him. "I miss her, too. But she is getting better. She's happier now. And we have to be happy about that, too."

20

Then one day, in January, 2015, Shannon asked if she could come to our house for a visit. We were surprised since she hadn't been there in over a year. I drove the forty-five-minute trip to her group home. On the way home, I told her that I never wanted her to feel trapped at our house. As soon as she needed to leave, I told her I would take her back home.

She lasted fifteen minutes. Then I drove her back to her group home. "I'm sorry, Mom," she said. "I thought I could come home, but I'm not ready yet."

"She said she was sorry!" I told Tom when I got home. For nine years I hadn't heard those words come out of Shannon's mouth. I was ecstatic.

The next time, she stayed two hours, and the next time, four. On that third visit, when she went outside to smoke, Martin grabbed the cigarette out of her mouth and crushed it with his foot. Too many times, he had heard me and Tom warn Shannon how bad smoking was for her health. "Don't smoke, Mom, it will make you sick," he said.

Later I explained to Martin. "Smoking comforts your mom. If you want her to feel like she is welcome here, you have to let her do what comforts her." I couldn't believe I could say those words.

Over the next couple of months, Shannon got increasingly better. She started to make eye contact with us. She started telling us about her classes. She started laughing again. She was glad to see us on her visits. She started calling me almost every day. She sent cards to her son. She visited her father.

To our amazement, in May of 2015, she found a part-time job cleaning at a local factory. Bringing home a paycheck, Shannon felt better about herself. Martin told her he was proud of her.

At first, she worked from 12 noon to 4 PM, three days a week. Then they asked her to work five days a week. Usually, someone from the group home would drive her to work, and she would walk the four miles back to the group home. When they changed her hours to 7 AM to 11 AM, Shannon struggled a little. She overslept, not hearing the two alarm clocks she had set. Her medications made it difficult for her to wake up. She would hurry out of the house, and at times forget to take her pills. Then they asked her to work six days a week. Afraid of losing the job, she agreed.

It was all too much too soon. Shannon hadn't worked in almost ten years. She started to get confused at work, and would come home saying that coworkers were making fun of her. She would call me up and tell me people were yelling at her.

At the end of July, after working almost four months, she walked to the Emergency Room and was admitted to the mental health floor of the hospital.

I didn't find out for three days. Worried, because I hadn't heard from Shannon, I called her counselor. "Shannon didn't want us to tell you that she's in the hospital," her counselor said.

Again, I could feel a cold chill running up my spine. What was I going to find when I visited her? Were we going to have to start all over again? Would she hate me again?

Going up in the elevator to visit her, I had to tell myself to breathe. Then I saw her. She walked up to me and gave me a hug. "I didn't want to bother any of you. I think I just needed to get my meds back in me. I'm probably getting out of here tomorrow."

21

It has been 18 months since the day we thought we had lost Shannon forever. On our living room wall, pictures of her before she became sick are still hanging: the tall dark-haired girl who was so pretty that she took my breath away. But I also have pictures of her now, missing teeth, short hair, but her eyes bright, laughing, sitting next to her son.

Attending her oldest brother's 40th birthday party in November, she sat in the kitchen with her siblings, laughing at the things they had done as kids. She said she was amazed that her brothers hugged her when she left. She said she thought they all hated her.

She wants to work again but says she's not quite ready yet. She volunteers at the local soup kitchen, saying it makes her feel good to help other people. She attends her classes that teach her about her illness, about how to cope with the voices.

The voices are still there. The hallucinations come and go. Just yesterday she said she thought she saw her son hanging out the window, crying and saying that everyone hated him. She called me up to make sure Martin had had a good day in school.

She says she wants to move into another apartment someday, but that she still needs the support of the counselors, who are in the group home twenty-four hours a day. She says someday she hopes to be able to help her son raise his children.

She often has the ability to laugh at the illness, something none of us could do for a long time. Just recently, I lost most of the vision in my right eye. I was driving Shannon back to the group home one day when it was snowing. "Wow. It's really hard to see today," I said.

"Do you want me to drive?" Shannon asked me.

"Oh, that would be great," I said. "I can't see, and you see things that aren't there!" We both started to giggle.

Shannon tells us about the voices now, and when we tell her they're not real, she is relieved. She's starting to believe us and trust us. Sometimes I see her outside, talking to herself and telling the voices she doesn't believe them anymore. When she comes back inside, she is calmer.

It is almost Christmas, and I have found myself singing the carols for the first time in many years. Shannon is going to her father's house on Christmas Eve and our house on Christmas Day. She told me she wants to be back at the group home by 4 PM, so she can celebrate Christmas with her friends in her home.

She doesn't remember many things about the past when she was so ill. She tells me that she was in hell, but she is not there anymore. I will probably never ask her to read this book; it would almost certainly scare her.

Her dad still gets Martin every other weekend, but now he also picks up Shannon. They stay at his house on Saturday during the day. He drives her to our house Saturday evening, where she spends the night with us. I drive her back to her home on Sunday. "That's my day to cook dinner," she tells us.

Her counselor told me, "Many of the families can't take the struggle, and they abandon the mentally ill. Many of our residents just let the disease take hold of them. They give up and just exist, but not your daughter. She is a fighter. She is a fighter."

Mental illness is an insidious, relentless disease. It withdraws hope and deposits fear.

Bob told us that most of the patients who live at Warren State Mental Institution will almost certainly live there until they die. Mental illness changes a person. The mentally ill person will probably never be the same as he or she was before the illness.

"Do you know what would save most of these people?" Bob asked me once. "If each person there had just one person who accepted him and loved him in spite of the changes, that person might get out of here."

It took us a very long time to learn that. But we know that now, Bob. We know.

SHADOW OF HERSELF

ABOUT THE AUTHOR

<u>A SHADOW OF HERSELF</u> is written by a registered nurse with over 25 years of nursing experience in both Pennsylvania and New York. Graduating Cum Laude with a degree in English from Penn State University, she started her nursing education after the birth of her fourth child. After graduating as Valedictorian from St. Vincent School of Nursing in Erie, Pennsylvania, she immediately became certified as an Emergency Nurse.

Work experience includes the following:

- Emergency Room Nurse
- Critical Care Dialysis Nurse
- Operating Room Nurse
- Director of Nursing
- Hospice Nurse Case Manager
- RN Supervisor for a Non-profit agency caring for the developmentally disabled

Her first book, <u>Midwife to the Other Side</u> tells the experiences of both family members and patients who shared glimpses of the other side, prior to and during their death.

Contact the author at
Midwifetotheotherside@yahoo.com